The Word

The Word

◇◇◇◇◇◇◇◇◇◇

CHRISTOPHER GALANO

RESOURCE *Publications* • Eugene, Oregon

THE WORD

Copyright © 2024 Christopher Galano. All rights reserved. Except for brief quotations in critical publications or reviews, no part of this book may be reproduced in any manner without prior written permission from the publisher. Write: Permissions, Wipf and Stock Publishers, 199 W. 8th Ave., Suite 3, Eugene, OR 97401.

Resource Publications
An Imprint of Wipf and Stock Publishers
199 W. 8th Ave., Suite 3
Eugene, OR 97401

www.wipfandstock.com

PAPERBACK ISBN: 979-8-3852-0742-8
HARDCOVER ISBN: 979-8-3852-0743-5
EBOOK ISBN: 979-8-3852-0744-2

04/19/24

Za Anu

Contents

Act I: The Word
The Word | 3
Envoi of the Word | 15

Act II: The Wandering
Petals | 25
The Moon Looks Lovely on You | 26
We Stand a Creek Apart | 29
The Piebald Bird | 30
Coronation | 32
As Wax on Leaves Repelling April Rain | 35
The Refuse | 36
A Vision | 38
The Evening Star | 40
Your Kingdom | 42
The Lady of the Mountain | 45
Delirium | 46
The Cave Mouth | 48

Act III: The Dying

The Wanderer | 51

Sunrise | 54

A Plum Tree at Summer's Start | 55

Death by Earth | 58

Little Gatherer | 59

On a Raft out on the Sea | 61

The Whirlpool | 62

Death by Water | 64

The Night's Fall | 65

A Zucchini Leaf After a Summer Rain | 70

Death by Air | 72

A Withered Rose | 73

The Body | 75

Death by Fire | 77

A Plum Tree at Summer's End | 78

The River Girl | 81

Act IV: The Becoming

Marching | 85

The Argument | 89

To the Villains at Fulfillment | 94

To the Youthful at Fulfillment | 96

To the Ancients at Fulfillment | 97

To the Prophets at Fulfillment | 99

The Becoming | 100

Act I:

The Word

THE WORD

Za Anu

I met a man who sang of lilies down-spiraling on a bier garden—
Who sang of ivory petals alighting ashen corpses and red dust—
Who sang of dancers kicking up red dust into the atmosphere—
Who sang of dancers banging glasses, splashing drinks on ashen corpses—
Who sang of dancers unaware of any lilies anywhere.
He offered me his spirit which was carried on the word.
Have you ever met a spirit that was carried on the word?
In the beginning was the Word.
I met a man who showed me the beginning.

Inside us grows a germ now broken from the primordial gyre, which eyed itself on static water and, coming of age, did not drown within the beauty of its own image.
Inside us grows a germ now spinning its own currents, which, strengthening, kills the fang-toothed, the snake-haired, to break from Mother's constricting care.
Inside us grows a clever germ erecting worlds of stone and steel and thought and word—
Worlds raised out of a gentle womb left razed within rotting encasements, entombed.
Inside us grows the lonely germ we have assumed.

And the lonely are contagious:
The paint-haired girl who summons mushrooms from her heart;
The wind-flared boy surpassing light inside a shopping cart;
The carrier of seeds who grows the bluebirds in the park—
All catch the germ and give a start—but acquiesce in turn while turning through their ages.

The Word

Abandoners of Self—they shuffle to the aegis of the skyscraper's
glitz and shine that blind the eye to wastage.
And the lonely ascend with momentum.
And the skyscraper ascends until inverted to a well that digs into
the mud of self-made expectation (although the fact, in time, is
forgotten),
Until the well runs deep and twirls not like gyres, yet still twirls
and, like fires, pulls a passerby toward the edge—
Then swirls a foot into the depth proclaimed as higher.
And the passerby, believing, goes on to preaching—
So congregate the lonely sty.
So learn to hate the lonely sty the foreign of their kind across the
sandy hills—
Watch how the wind makes play of grains upon the sandy hills!—
Hate them for their foreign word, for if in the beginning was
the word, then foreign word means foreign beginning, means
foreign existence counts for sinning.
Hence the wars and eager wills for winning even dust.

The hate flies too at foreign words born local:
The lonely sty stay lonely, subject
To the common mud but never
Guaranteed by it: the lonely sty
Stay lonely, and loneliness only multiplies.
And every entity pursues its own
Preservation—between the common streets
And roofs and words and personalities—
And at times between us.
The lonely sty is an ancient story of home-
Grown hope to plunge the roots
Beneath the mud and shoot the leaves
Into the sky, to join what we have gained
With what we've lost in swirling with
The sty—and of killing that hope before
Admission. Do you hear it? The story
Echoes forward toward us, happens

Act I: The Word

Now, around us, listen as

Hand drops hammer strikes nail pierces palm
Against the wood that shakes the balm
From the surface of the earth like dew
Flung from bowing petals by an early-risen shrew.

The shrews and scoundrels and Pharisees bark
Their hatred for the One who had come to save them.
They had rallied for death—death to their
Oppressors—death they chanted in their caves
And in their fantasies. And *Death
To the Romans* turned with ease to *Death
To Jesus of Nazareth*, when he by
Temple baths refused the violent cry
And washed instead the mud from blind
But willing eyes—that chant condemning them
Along the Sorrowful Way as

Hand drives hammer strikes nail pierces feet
Against the wood that stirs the fiends from their seats
In the flames of the pit blessed by Satan's conceit,
Like us; they come hold witness in the dust.

Dust swirls where they step through the crowd,
Flickering between two realms, felt as a prick
In the heart of the shrew that throws the sorrows
Of her nightly abuse upon the Man to grow
Her hatred by it; a breath blown on the scoundrel's
Soul that casts the daily guilt of his failings
Upon the Man to urge his mockeries for it;
A whisper of the scripture in the mind
Of the Pharisee that sustains the claim
Of heresy to assuage his doubts of it;
And heard as a stray pig's many-voiced squeals
That call the lesser devils waiting at

The Word

Realm's edge for the Man's death
To make their own accursed homes upon
This downcast earth—a hope now spurred as

Hands lift cross lifts Man and slides in earthen slot
That keeps him raised above the land—
His body jolting, the nails holding—his stand
For having taught them to be perfect like God.

His followers have scattered—
Fled through sandy hills before the funeral choirs.
O bless those ones who held their step at Calvary!

Black clouds clap thunder over the crowd:
While the lightning, dim by the light of Jesus' heart, yet blinding to poor eyes, cracks a throwing-stone and draws its viscid blood which flows the Sorrowful Way until reaching the Temple—
Up the stonework steps and through the archway entrance; then onto the High Priest's throne, now vacant, while a gale throws his finest robes before the cross.
He lifts his arms to block the gust that blows directly through his heart, that chills the jeerers' mockeries midair, unsettling the crowd dispersing in fear:
The thunder claps overloud:
And a soldier seized by panic sends his spear through rib-bare flesh—
Then genuflects beneath fluorescent blood and limpid water which shower the penitent, shower the dust, and overgleam the stone blood stream until the Temple's empty throne.
Jesus throws his spirit on the word and throws his word toward the heavens: "It is accomplished."
His head drops while white lightning strikes the cross, traverses spring-well heart, runs rose-glowing stream, and at the Temple cracks unholy stonework seams:

Act I: The Word

The fissure traces back, splitting the path apart, and swallows the fertilizing stream, and swallows the terror-playing fiends, and swallows their unbelieving screams at the sight of the wood where lightning holds its form attached to heaven:
Leaves reach from wooden arms to feed on light of higher realms reflected in the sheen of blackening, closing clouds, amid high trumpets singing triumph through the cracking, thunderous sounds:
A lily blossoms at the tip, electric with the charge, reflected infinite in every realm as highest art:
The beings of higher realms gaze struck by highest art.
The roots have meanwhile plunged from base of wood through sand to draw the charge of places where the good of Man gives way to raw abasement in the form of snakes that coil and always gnaw the realms of Underland—
The charge now feeding lightning held from either end—
The axis on which all the world has come to spin—
Illumining human eyes perceiving holy light:
The final light soon vanished as black consumes the sky.

Soldiers bow before their duties: hands
Once firm to lift the cross now quaver wildly.
Mary his Mother, sole one steady,
Swathes his body in his manger robes,
And, still steady, perceiving holy light,
Holds his rainy, whip-lashed body
Soon to resurrect.

I met a man who sang of lilies free-falling for three days—
Who sang of open petals piling upon supine corpses, settling lofty dust—
Who sang of sable-sandaled dancers leaving dust upon the ground—
Who sang of sable-sandaled dancers pouring drinks on supine corpses—
Who sang of all libations beading off the shroud of lilies.

The Word

He shared forbidden words arranged within forbidden orders.

Inside us grows a germ now broken from the basement laboratories where walls buzz sterile white, pipe bulbs lighting like neither sun nor moon.
Inside us grows a germ composed of Nature's elements—healthy in her own proportions, healthy by her own intent—but twisted out of form; mixed with demoniacs, malice, and discontent.
Inside us grows a germ that passes on the word that it begets, spinning syllables buzzing after its pattern, low-wave and warbled—long-range interference—buzzing the air in tune, and through our ears so our hearts too, which though not easily infected are so frequently inflicted by the song.
Our hearts, low-buzzing, echo the germ-spun word, and, first through fervor, then habit, we learn only to speak it, or else we cover our mouths.
Look how we all cover our mouths:
Masks for every patient in line, standing indifferently—foot out-flung, back half-slouched, fists pocketed—bored of waiting.
And look—down there—how one man lifts his hand to his mask—only to scratch his eye; then drops his hand and sighs.
Listen to their hearts buzzing as low as their sighs.
And listen! Listen to the sudden beating: hearts off-rhythm and rushed—only to keep the pace at the guard's push, the stutter steps quick-fading to a halt.
See the complacency of those who trade their agency for preservation!
See how the lab-germ latches onto the germ we are known by!
Observe how the manufactured co-opts the organic!

And notice, there, the man who watches
His watchers—and there! He breaks from the line
For the horizon! Away from the setting sun!
Arriving then by rover to the line's front,
Where tents eat every person in turn,
Before released toward the skyscrapers,

Act I: The Word

Star-speckled black against the rosy burn,
New city promised and begun.

—A promise of vast relations that erode those between us.
I have known the promised relations only between us, when we
  interwove our bodies like the electrical filament interweaving
  the galaxies: that perfect tapestry.
—A promise of speed that separates us, so that we meet in the
  same time but misaligned from the rush.
I have known progress at your touch, when the ancient youth of a
  new moon reflected on your skin and tuned my heart aligned:
  that illicit pale blush.
—A promise of transformation by bestowal, only to those who
  acquiesce.
I have known transformation when we harmonized our chests,
  and our limbs flashed as one with the burning comet above:
  that cosmic love-tangle.
I have known the sterile light, the deep shadows underneath
  strained eyes, the bowed heads and hunched backs for code
  that finds the code that finds, but so removed never reveals;
Known the sterile voices, the formulaic rhyme, the cheap glitter
  and the tampered bodies, the scentless, touchless, tasteless,
  where senses atrophy and die, and a heart knowing joy only
  from virtual disguise designed to steal;
Known the stolen moments when a heart so rhythmed never
  noticed heartbeats calling, for the low-buzz rhythm resonated
  with the falling, falling, falling out of fields.
Technology is not our final yield but a cocoon to life-support our
  spirits through transfiguration.
Reject the buzz heart-tuning as the germ-spun word to trap us
  midway formed.
We shed our shells by daybreak: no night lasts forever.

In dreams I've seen our butterflied kind on forever's other side:
Man and Woman high-resonant, heaven's dimensions worn as
  halos, plants grown at will, raised from rippling hills, hills

The Word

themselves raised up, a lily bush blossoming then dying into
  itself to blossom again, spun by the swipe of a wrist:
Songs lifting bricks, building heart-tuned cities,
Songs lifting waves over cliffs to water the gardens,
Songs to lift our bodies with.
I see our daughter singing with arms uplifted in the garden,
  singing the flowers and vegetables into bloom, singing the
  world alive.
This is why I beg you, belly full with baby, keep aligned your
  heart: keep sovereign your wrist.
We may starve in the dust, lost of paths and savings, faceless to
  society, nameless to friends and family:
May forgiving graces save us from our pangs when there are no
  oases—
I see no oases—wind itself wailing—

Watch how the wind makes play of grains upon the sandy slopes!
Reshaping desertscape as ocean waves, rolling, shave the coast!
Look at the glints of gold
The sunset throws on the land,
That holy promise of tomorrow
Awaiting our fulfilling!

I met a man who sang of lilies white-
Shining in the night, heaven-
Haloed petals lifting rested
Corpses shedding all their dust;
And feet of dancers snapping to—
A sudden start—as dancers
Drop their glasses, lose
Their drinks before the corpses—
All the dancers cower at the glowing art of lilies.

He reassured of humankind's full arc.
We wandered prodigals through history.
We finish with a choice: accept the mark

Act I: The Word

Of the beast or spurn false-promised bliss to free
The spirit from cocoon and turn the flesh
Angelic, so, like moons, it can reflect
The light of Source. Once solid walls turn to mesh
And ripple in the wind. Upon the wrecked
Womb, fertile till its death, that light of Source
Dances in spotted step. Our task: to tear
The mesh of our cocoons, let the full force
Of light inside, receive the sacred glare.
We'll burn all residue of former sin.
We'll align, axes: on us worlds will spin.

We wandered prodigals to set our roots
In fertile mud, to draw the nourishment,
To feed the green and faithful, fragile shoots
Of our spirits. As from manure's fresh scent
Rise fresher flowers wafting bolder yet,
We must transfigure what is crude and base
To highest form, illumining the earthly set,
We only able 'cause we know the face
Of darkness: that face is ours: we are the beast
That ravages then cools its pulsing veins
In putrid mud; we too the angel, least
Among the heavenly bodies with an aim
Past them: heaven and hell battle in our blood,
One raising us, one lowering, through the mud.

There are powers that would bind us to the mud
And suck the moisture, turning all to dust.
They are wolves in lambskin chewing on the cud
Of dark old dreams whose false façades they thrust
On many. Many accept for knowing not
Or fearing worse—or love of their children—love
The wolves know not: the wolves, with teeth half rot,
Devour our children, then in body gloves
They throw the bones. And they will burn the bones,

The Word

Succeeding for some time, but their success
Will stand on self-made dust and dust alone—
Watch how the wind makes play of dust!—caressed
By grains, the many will grasp at sandy walls,
Each lonely, separated, from the fall.

We wandered separate so that we could learn
To carry crosses, to forgive the givers
Of crosses, to forgive ourselves—to burn
Cracked shells, throw ashes into teardrop rivers.
Why feel shame for flourishing? Evolving, we
Butterfly our peers and very earth. We break
Apart to put together consciously.
Transcend the entranced, the enchanter, and the snake
Whose protest points are valid but distracted.
We wandered separate so that we could map
Our hearts within this plane. Pain reenacted
For manufactured dreams, or market cap,
Or half-formed thought, serves hardly to remit.
Forget the smoke: aim at the ultimate.

Be flame, be ash, be ember and new spark!
Pass through familiar death and live again.
Be wave, be splash, be eddy and deep dark!
That void of death is an illusory end.
Be the leaf losing grip when it is withered!
Pass through familiar death for birth again
Of fertile soil when suns endow fair weather.
A clutching life makes death appear the end
On fallen boughs suspended over dirt.
Remember death: remember rebirth again.
Be flowing as warm wind against your hurt!
Be flowing as desert wind without an end!
Remember death? In light you are born again.
Don't clutch life: you are life: you do not end.

Act I: The Word

You are blessed and whole. You are love. You are gold—
Containing and contained by Source: look in
Your soul and put your cross in earthen hold:
Straighten your spine, send roots into your sin,
Transmute their force, send shoots into the sky,
Forgive who wronged you for they do not know—
Thank those who wronged you for rights in disguise:
Manure for soil on which your spirit grows.
Draw lightning from your heart to burn the germs
That feed upon your spirit. Launch that light
Into the heavens. Yoke the newly earned
With the long lost, preparing for the night.
Allow the lily blossom with full rays
From your crown. Come: we will dawn the new days.

I met a man who sang of lilies more
Beauteously arrayed than our Solomons,
Layered petals clothing risen corpses, giving drink
Unto the dust; and feet of dancers halting hushed
Wherever they stand; and dancers without glasses,
Without drinks, all living corpses turned to stone
Before Woman and Man wearing lilies.

I met a man whose spirit calibrated mine, his spirit carried on the word, the word that tunes the heart just as the germ, just as the buzz, though born through us of Source, tunes us aligned.
The course of history plays as music, so, see how the cycles rhyme, rebirthing old wisdom with new intelligence, rebuilding latest systems out of ancient ashes, see how the word spins the world on worthy spines.
The melody of our new days now echoes back from the foothills—an anthem we will make our own—to wrap the world around our spines and round our daughter's—though born under shadows, her notes will usher new light, her arias will raise half-lidded eyes, she will chorus the world alive.

The Word

Until that hour we wreathe the world with golden-glimmering ribbons, ribbons endless as our wedding rings: we will chime with the fluent wind—jive to the new song—and O we will, when we speak—at last—sing!

ENVOI OF THE WORD

While spires triple-braidedly arose from the sand
Like a grove of pigtails standing on their ends,
I strode among the half-buried ruins beyond the hill.
A man of marble stood upon a spire-peak,
His robes appearing to flow as sand,
His hand pointing east, his head missing.

An ibis settled on the neck, black
From neck to beak, white-feathered
Chest-down until the feet, black feet
Absorbed by ruffling feathers as
The bird made comfortable his seat,
Holding his beak westward.

I followed the beakline to westward where
The sand had parted unto sea, revealing a wide city
In slumber underneath, unremembered by
The city builders. The city shimmered gold
In light that breached the restless sea,
Where fish shimmered and made the city home.
The city stood as home inside the future waves
Flowing past us—will stand again within the era
We have known. So said the Lady of the Sea.

She'd ambled onto shore until beside me,
Her wet-fitting, long-trailing, turquoise dress
Brushing the ocean on the sand, a path of mosses
Growing after her. She flashed your eyes and raised
A single brow in self-assurance, her hair
Marble-smooth as yours, though, while drying, curling
Into rings. "Come, come," she said, her hand
Upon my shoulder with a touch like yours also.

The Word

Behind me the desert had carried the spires off.
My path to you, once clear, was lost.

*

"So, so it is sweet to go beneath the waves.
O sauna that desert! Come, now, my love,
You will breathe freely beneath the waves;
They are my own. O walk as when you walk
On land—though slow, the current behind
Will carry you, the current which I blow.

"Do not fear the guards at the gates:
They are waiting for me. They lower arms
At my request. I'll tell them that I come
With the man who travels west. Their spears
Will rise again protecting you as all
The city. Come! And I will show you
The one who will offer what he can."

*

"This way, this way, into the street
Of scuffless gold; hardly any turn
Here without need, and who could need
Within these city walls? Come, come,
Another turn: his house is numberless.
You see the golden numbers on the walls?
You see the wall without a number or a bell?
Come! You must knock and call his name.
You must speak as freely as you breathe."

"His name," I said, my voice the first
Time travelling through water as through air;
"What is his name?" "He goes by the name
Of his visitor," she answered. I raised my hand

Act I: The Word

Toward the door. Hesitating, I asked her:
"Why are you doing this for me?" "Because
In doing this for you, I do it for myself."
Triple-knocking on the door, I called my name.

Triple-counting foot-taps, I had waited.
The door had opened inward; inward the current
Pulled us, in toward the shadows fading by
A golden light once we had come inside—
A rasping voice then welcoming our time.

*

"When you are made to choose, will you favor yourself?
Toward all those you love, will you expand yourself?
When the many will call you a liar, will you believe yourself?"

"I will."

"I give you the flame." He struck
A match against his palm to spark
A fire beneath the waves.
I thanked him but confessed
My cashless, creditless state,
Having refused the mark.

"O Amorismo: Amorocrazia!
Currency is trust; we built our own on love.
Consider Circe, under Odysseus' sword, promising her bed.
Consider the riches gained as though he'd carried equal treasures.
Consider her fate if she had ever betrayed.
So they devised their currency.
With the Lady you have come as though with numberless
   treasures.
You and I sow the new trust."

The Word

"Who will maintain tabs?"

"We will: we don't forget our love."

"What if a memory is lost?"

"Receptive hearts will make new memories, harder to make
   disappear than bits stored on a drive—erasure is inevitable.
Trust rebuilding more than memories."

"Circe—she offers her bed—
A guiding story stoking debauchery."

"Love is panoramic: expand your ken on love."

*

A pair of twins quibbled, arms
Windmilling, voices siren-sounding,
Veins in foreheads pounding
To the rhythm—one wearing a silver
Breastplate and helmet bouncing
The subsea sunlight onto sand,
A scarlet cape and tufted feathers
Waving with the rhythm—and
The other wearing only a long white robe
While currents lifted copper hair
Jerking and pulsing—an aureole of rhythm.

They turned to us ecstatic for an audience.
The Lady of the Sea, brow cocked in her
Anticipated boredom, glided to a sitting-rock
Beside us, thighs crossed high and eyes
Toward the horizon-spanning lake in elegant
Indifference. Alone I heard the passions of the twins,
The armored speaking, then the robed, in turn.

Act I: The Word

"Young flesh, straight arrows, leaping bile: the image
Of the soldier slain in battle-glory
And the sweet lady kneeling by the wreckage,
Giving his final drink—that is the peak
Of achievement—that is man's height of expression
Beyond the need or ability of the word."

"The hummed, the sung, the dialectic word
Of villainy and redemption eclipses the image
In richness and exactness of expression.
By layers of music and meaning does the glory
Of the human soul approach the cloud-crowned peak:
By this is man recovered from the wreckage."

"Misunderstanding delivered the wreckage
Of nations duped by the ambiguous word.
Even where dictionaries match, the peak
Is clouded by a poor description. The image
Of the mountain assures our common glory
For we are visual beings, favoring visual expression."

"The animal favoring of visual expression
Promoting basest inclinations—the wreckage
Of the soul results from such false forms of glory.
By higher orders is man endowed with the word
Which raises him through ages, while the image
By lower orders, entertaining away from the peak."

"The sculpted clay and swift-stroked paint of the peak:
The highest known as modest matter—expression
Perfected in living, realm-traversing image
Layers clearly, regardless of cultural wreckage,
The music and meaning even of the word,
Yet moving also the corporeal glory."

The Word

"If man will seek his soul's impending glory
He needs which medium shows the peak
Always—that of his own begotten word,
Weightless and lifting, matterless expression
Rebirthing readily among the wreckage
To most precisely form a guiding image."

"Young man, speak! Do you favor the word or the image?"
"The peak of achievement or cause of the wreckage?"
"Which is the glory of expression?"

"The glory of expression is the act.
The act is what the image and the word
Both indicate—to manifest the heard
And seen through brimming intention, most exact
Of motions. Valuable as proper guides
These two projections of our kind—expressing,
Though, what high fact? Space shrinks and hours are pressing—
Just how will man achieve the other sides?
The act is the real point—when human heart
Is swollen by the filling of the soul,
And body has accorded with the whole
Of the earth. By action the man, though as small part,
Raises the final peak from humble knoll:
The world is stage and canvas, life the highest art."

The twins relaxed their arms, their hair
And feathers resting in the currents, and parted
To let me pass, revealing the single-sail boat
Shore-marooned and manned by a wispy sailor.

*

"Although you hear these whispers round my bones,
My spirit speaks aloud. I belong to the Lady now:
She is exquisite, even when unravelling

Act I: The Word

Our lifethreads in the flash before the snip.
She always keeps all well beneath the waves.
While I pull the ropes, she will ferry us on.
Rest now, son, in the shadow of the sail."

*

I woke inside the boat. The marble hand then
Pulled me over bow to risen sand, where spires
Had turned to stumps. Sand swirled, hummed,
Then rose to chants of *Hosanna in Excelsis*,
Harmonies rippling sand-grains inward, consuming.
The ibis cried and beat his wings, unmoving.
All died in one brown downing of the desert.
O let us thaw all souls while we march nightward,
Igniting twirling torches with the one last match of Christ!
O let us stride for west, striving lightward!

Act II:

The Wandering

PETALS

While buyers and their sellers bustle and call
Through burdened-beastly howls and short-cut squeals,
Wide red and yellow petals softly fall

On polyester canopies of stalls,
And whittled wooden goods, and bergamot peels,
As though no man or beast had let out calls,

And on the boy unable to see all
His path, who on his rusty brakes had reeled
And, having pedaled nimbly through the fall

Of footsteps, nearly missed the girl with shawl
Of coral on her head, and eyes of teal,
And voice not backing any market calls,

And steered instead into the stall-high wall
Of flower crates, breaking the boards and seals,
As he who peddled them gaped at the fall

Of his petals. And the boy, quick to crawl
Out from the mess toward the girl's bare heels,
Through the unceasing buyer-seller calls,
Holds up to her the flowers whose petals fall.

THE MOON LOOKS LOVELY ON YOU

The moon looks lovely on you, love—its silver
Aura on your skin dyed golden from
The noonday sun; its mute light mirrored on
Your ocean-salted, marble-smooth, cocoa-flavored
Hair; its full and sacred orb suspended
In the warm and eager, amber-gleaming
Syrup of your eyes—and I had dreams
Of this same night but never could remember
Them on waking, lest I might profane
The image taking it through day's routines
And worldly worries—never could till now,
When worlds have fallen away, and you float dressed
In that long prophesied attire against
This velvet darkness sprinkled with the stars.

Act II: The Wandering

Mountain wheat
Flowing over the horizon—
Our daily bread.

The Word

Over the crowded laughter
The poet on the hill enunciates
The red of a rosebud.

WE STAND A CREEK APART

We stand a creek apart that spans an ocean,
And send our rafts directly on the waves.
Your raft, adorned in silver jewels and joys,
Breaks the white waves that slap the bow and clap,
Reaching my shore unscathed. I take each jewel
And under sun and moon admire the shine
And clarity; I decorate my space
On this eroded bank in this lost time.

And my raft wants the spirit and the earth
To catch the wind and break the plashing water.
Much gold slips through, unnoticed, to the depths;
And what arrives, if it arrives, you take
And wonder, I am sure, why you have endowed
So much, and whether I will meet your height.

THE PIEBALD BIRD

A tap, and a tap, and a tap, and a soaring screech—
The piebald bird makes known her bursting wish
To burst from the bars and eaglelike to fish
In the teal stream rushing beyond her reach—
To take the salmon by the head and lift
It shimmering to the layered radiant rings
Of the sun: for that she beats her cage-wide wings
And peers out dancing side to side and swift.

Watchers will question her species and build, and speak
Of the audacity to challenge her mold—
The bird will oversing them with gaping beak,
Call freedom to their own hunched birds as they scold—
They will, in cowardice, clamp their cages, but weak:
All birds will, by cleverness, break from their cages—unfold!

ACT II: THE WANDERING

High tide—
Breakers on the rocks
Glimmer.

CORONATION

Twisting living branches by the square:
Closing round amid the mockeries
Within unknown worship of a higher
Order: the soldiers prick the flesh and look

For blood—a droplet spilled, a healthy stream.
The beaten accedes, though eyes avert. The hunger
Had drained the vigor, thirst had withered limbs,

Long ago. Who could reject? The fitting
Readjusted, repositioned, thorns
Abounding in wide asymmetry: the bodies
Bow by the imperial coronation.

Act II: The Wandering

The birds' morning song—
The poppy flower bowing
By the weight of dew.

The Word

Honeybees abrush
Among the clover flowers
In the backyard lawn.

AS WAX ON LEAVES REPELLING APRIL RAIN

As wax on leaves repelling April rain,
So may you gather into feeble beads
The questioning and mockeries and spite
Of those who care the less for you for each
Suspicion offered at their lofty altars—
What secrets linger underneath the damasked
Altars?—gather and fling toward the puddles
Upon the clay, which bear the iron chimes
And songs of the new days—fling them away
Until the clay has moistened, and the roots,
And every leaf has swollen; then, unbending,
Stand adorned with the fury's gilded gleam
Against the Book's last stories, as the sporting
Cherubs have long rehearsed—unbending stand,
Remembering, and vast-surrounded by,
The Holy Many who were persecuted first.

THE REFUSE

Steel swells with silent shouldering of mobs;
Exudes their breath toward the breathless blue,
The city ash adorning every pretty splash
Of advertisement. Turn your hope toward
The future: we have made it today.

A plastic bag has crossed the valley on
A wind-hint that had picked it from the balcony.
What sacred face, hidden even to the wearer,
Will ignore the triumph? Those voices call
That were ignored or once acknowledged—
Refusal once undoes the former good.

Come, my assassins, sprinkle your iron confetti
Until your fingers tire—then I will be ready
To welcome you, as you will be ready for receiving.
Come—and beware who proclaim to behave in your
Interest: they probably speak in their favor.

Binary digits and major fifths transmitted from
The leaderboards: what phony gods will interface
Today? Will they respond? And share our taste?
Are they those plants who have grown mouths
And crawl like insects out of starships?
Revere the spirit, man! Must man revere
While bent? Will gods be reverent too?

When I am dead I want a buried grave,
Where I may mingle with the guileless worms
And kiss the fallen apples of your womb.

Act II: The Wandering

Moon beyond the streetlight,
Star beyond the moon:
Orion's sword, fallen—

A VISION

A vision through the blinding of the river's piercing glare,
Beyond the watchful sparrows and the sun's unbreaking stare:
A daughter in the meadow sitting with the daffodils
And weaving, without plucking, living flowers through her hair.

Act II: The Wandering

Evening wind—
A leaf is blown from its branch,
A leaf is lifted up.

THE EVENING STAR

The evening star white-sparkles in the syrup of your eye,
That evening sky long cleared of any traces of the rain.
How wide has grown the edging of your spirit's windowpane!
How deep how grown the well that holds the darkness and the
    light!

And I perceive no future in the blankness: all is void
And without any sign that I can glean or spell or count.
Remember when we climbed through breathless midnight up the
    mount?
Remember at the peak with newfound breaths our lips were
    joined?

So wherein lies my doubt? Within what tremble of the earth?
I have looked long about the fissures crawling up our house;
I have spent hours in our bedroom routing out the spies.

And I have seen you waver in your motions; yet you sing.
What constellations do you witness mirrored with your image?
Perhaps you're more discerning as a reader of the skies.

ACT II: THE WANDERING

Roof-cast shadow!
The maple bough shivers—
Dark-veined leaves and opaque.

YOUR KINGDOM

There grows a purple flower in the grasses,
Sway-dancing with the wind that every afternoon passes
Across the mountain's ocean-looking field:
May the vine be as our sword, and the petals as our shield!

And may the scent provide to those who wander
A compass for their energies so frequently so squandered,
As they traverse the hallways of their minds,
Turning over ashtrays and gnawing at the rinds.

And when you beam exalted melodies
From out of shattered plates and throughout a shattered realm,
May we who hear regain the strength to sing them.

And when you disappear all villainies,
Remaking a new world with your crown to serve as helm,
May I be but a leaf within the orchards of your Kingdom.

Act II: The Wandering

These garden ashes—
The red rising sun
Turns clementine.

The Word

Three Sisters—
The dust of drought swirls
Among the evergreens.

THE LADY OF THE MOUNTAIN

Crag-sent hollers over sand and hours:
    Cascading notes.
The Lady of the Mountain rages through crystalline wind.
Collapsing rocks keep count:
    Our melodies, too, woven in.
The Lady of the Mountain whirls hysteria:
    Our dance steps, too, begin.
As earth folds over sand, time folds over hours:
    Our breaths, then, raging, spin.
The Lady of the Mountain rages, raising up her breasts.
Let us raise her notes.
Let us give her rest.

DELIRIUM

Give me your hand, release your care
By dancing feet to whirling air.
A step apart, a step toward—
That's what the open desert's for.

Hand on your hip from under sheer
Rounding, revolving, like new worlds,
And pulling sand and hours near
Till mixed and melded and refurled.

We move across unmoving space, unturning time
Within your shawl's enclosing walls: your eyebeams stun
Translucent flesh, exposing mind—

And so we'll move as two made one
Until we've sung the desert sun
A-fee-foe-fum delirium!—
Until we've sung the desert sun
A-fee-foe-fum delirium!

An airy lift, no seconds turned,
A stepwise shift, an old world burned.
A little seed, unleashed by flame,
Sprouts in the earth of rhyming name.

Cheek on your cheek, chest on your chest,
By magnet's sway the lightning cracks
And speeds the heartbeat from its rest,
Igniting shawl around our backs.

We move within our trifold light: your eyebeam moon
Mixed with the star mixed with the lightning: three made one
As midnight mingles with the noon—

Act II: The Wandering

And so we'll move the lighted run
Until we've sung the desert sun
A-fee-foe-fum delirium!—
Until we've sung the desert sun
A-fee-foe-fum delirium!

Does one make half, non-dual the whole?
Lies soul in body or body in soul?
A dress's swirl reveals the answers.
There is none like you among the dancers.

By merging light, veins humming tones,
The pupils widen, hair grows long
And waves the patterns of our bones:
Our bodies rising as new song.

Our bodies rising form the gyre: that early gyre
That births the stars and brews the promises to come,
Unfurling on electric wires—

And so we'll turn not two or one
As we have sung the desert sun
A-fee-foe-fum delirium!—
As we have sung the desert sun
A-fee-foe-fum delirium!

THE CAVE MOUTH

The cave mouth gapes at the arrival of our kind:
An ancient yawn of elder boulders—
Will you come with me inside?
I feel the airs along my wrist;
They cool the blood and chill the wish,
But there is fire in the sky.
And I have brought a candle,
And it glows along the wick;
And we have both the breath
To stoke it to a guide:
And stoke it to our warmth,
And stoke it as the sky.
Around that corner, barely lit,
The tunnel turns toward the night;
But we have gone through many,
Heralding the dawns;
And when the candle tires out,
Our songs will serve as light.

Act III:

The Dying

THE WANDERER

She wanders where the willows weave their branches into braids,
Along the pond with the black swan that leaves the lucid wake.
I hear the footsteps on the grasses. Do you hear the footsteps?
Those are not her footsteps on the grasses: the grasses part the way,
As she within her reverie, and with a sparrow on her shoulder,
Sings of present blooms, and future fruits, and when the wind was colder.
Do you hear the footsteps through the unremembered pastures?
That crunch the drying grasses into pale and flattened wake?

She wanders where the pond releases drink into the rivers,
And wanders where the rivers weave their streams in triple braids.
The fishes rise to greet her at the surface of the water,
And splash to match her melody, a harmony of waves.
The metronome beats steadily, a little distance farther,
And every step sends tremors through the forest's underways.
Electric mushrooms read the shakes and tell them to the trees,
Which spread their leaves and crowd their branches, joining canopies.
The late spring sun appears as gone to him who walks through trees.

She wanders where the rivers give their drink into the sea,
And stands upon the pebbles, shaped and smoothed by many tides,
And looks toward horizon where a burning moon arises,
Appearing as a second sun to light her melodies.
And do you see her song?
It ripples as the ocean waves throughout the atmosphere,
And glistens as the violet vapors of her subtle soul,

The Word

And carries scents of flower-blends to those with hearts to hear;
And those who wash beneath her song,
And loose their hair, and let it long,
Their ravaged flesh turns whole.
And do you feel the footsteps? Marching to the waves?
She also feels the footsteps following her way.
She turns into the forest where her song diffuses through,
And moves according to the sight her song provides.

He walks toward the pebbled shore, the man with iron joints,
And raises hands to block the moon in thinking it the sun,
And falls onto his creaking knees, lets waves onto his lap,
Allows the rising tide to raise him, turn him on his back,
And carry him from land, and pull him swiftly undersea;
And iron feels as autumn leaves when falling undersea.
And undersea runs overland, in yearning for the moon,
And grinds the pebbles down to sand, and pulls the remnants home,
And splashes back onto itself, and gives a droplet to a leaf.

Act III: The Dying

Midnight winds
Whip rain against the window—
A fig leaf quavers.

SUNRISE

Pale ruby seeps throughout the sable shroud extending
Across the sleeping city softly stirring in her dreams.
The silhouettes of evergreens cut through the morning burn,
A tearing in the tapestry along the secret seams.

Some motion in the streets: some stir themselves to waking,
And wander by the rivers that run mirrors of the air.
And some admire the solemn beauty of the ceaseless streams;
To halfway-lidded eyes, a ruby shines as diamond-fair.

And some the more discerning, being long now river-stained,
Move wearily in sadness that diverges into wrath,
In search for balm or outlet that will soothe their doubling pain.

Their rumbling shakes the earth, as do the jitters of police,
Opposing marks converging on the city's central path:
The swell of revelation tempts to break the morning peace.

A PLUM TREE AT SUMMER'S START

Encircled by the flickering of fireflies
That wanderingly pulse beneath the tired evening skies,
You shower down the petals of your blooms,
The rouge-tipped porcelain reflecting hidden lights,
And phasing under shadows as though each an earthly moon.
Your cousin stands a stump in front of you,
Consumed by rot and negligence, then pared to half its size.
And you have also worn those signs of rot,
The knuckled-growths extending down and weighing down
Your branches. Again we knew and yet we have forgotten.
Again we knew yet asked of you, "Will you give fruit this year?"
And though you know you cannot give the answer.
And though you know it all, you do not waver without wind,
But send among the fireflies your gentle petals' spin.

The Word

White-peppered soil,
Young basil—the memory
Of a poisoned mouse.

Act III: The Dying

Beneath zucchini shade,
This golden morning beaming—
A rat-feast for maggots!

DEATH BY EARTH

Dirt, embraced, and embracing, seeps in through
The little gashes, opened wider by
The sweat, within the dermis. Worms, writhing,
Pierce afterward, and bore new holes inside
Also. The pulsing arms do not writhe, not
Beneath the weight: twitch, and cry, and gnashing
Here—pressure stays all of man's action. Eye-
Lids stretch vestigial where, within this last
Rest, soil, which grew, consuming now, compacts
And blankets desperate eyes, the searching hopes
All silenced. Breath is gone from him; ghost, given
Up. Body relaxed, it spills out into
The caress, merging the opposing kinds,
Opposed no longer. Flesh, transformed, becomes

Earth's own, and draws a fallen seed inside,
Consoling and bedewing. And the seed
At once, known, knowing—having wisdom—cracks
Its shell to sweep the dwelling, reaches out
Its eager vine—an emerald dawning. Rain,
Decay, and mineral, conspire to nurse
The youthful shoot, the flesh transforming once
More, donning a new life. And, with force, and
With wisdom, Earth breaks through her very own
Rind—damaged and recovering, in one
Twined motion. There, at last, the Earth breathes wind,
And feeds directly on the sun, in time
To feed the others, growing of their own.
Flesh, of dirt, and returning, cycles through . . .

LITTLE GATHERER

The white of your feathers is showing,
O little gatherer of twigs!
And where are you taking the clippings?
What secret shelter have you long been preparing?
The trembling has been growing in the soils.
The efforts have been building for the tearing away
Of the laid roads and olden houses.
How quick you turn your neck!
How subtle your perception of the motions!
May your protection keep you with the strength of many bricks!
May tremble-drummers fumble as though held by wilted sticks!

The Word

Sudden black summits
Over these low brick houses—
A raindrop strikes a leaf.

ON A RAFT OUT ON THE SEA

A multitude has gathered on a raft out on the sea,
For they had loved the water, even on the battered raft.
A tidal wave arises from horizon at their backs;
But they refuse to interrupt their chanting of the sea.
Their hope is in the walk, and then the run, across the water.
But they do not believe that such a power comes to man.
And what is one to say? A word is unconvincing.
And what is one to do? Is one to dance upon the waves?
To light instead a stronger love that pulls to water-dancing?
And how is one to dance, when so many won't be saved?

THE WHIRLPOOL

I

Whirling, twirling, swishing round,
        The waters form the funnel.
The people leaping from the ground
        Go diving through the tunnel.

They feared the land and how it shook!
They worshipped water, so they took
        Their jumps into the funnel.

Where does it lead in pulling down?
Do zealots never fear to drown
        When going through the tunnel?

II

Whirling, twirling, swishing round,
        I throw a rope to sea.
Take hold! I'll pull you to the ground!
        What ravaged looks at me!

They loathed the rope as much as land,
And spurned the help away with hand
        That plunged into the sea.

How quick the mind can be to turn!
How swift the heart to newly burn!
        How sharp the back to me!

Act III: The Dying

III

Whirling, twirling, swishing round,
      I tie the rope to dock.
What roaring, soaring, crashing sounds!
      How feeble was the talk!

I jump into the peopled water,
After visions of a daughter.
      Hold me, rope, to dock!

How light the body on the stream
That swallows those inclined to scream
      And chokes those apt to talk!

IV

Whirling, twirling, swishing round:
      A mind in swelling waves!
I look toward the lilies found
      At dock, the hope to save!

The lily-bearer at the pier
Is striving with the rope to steer
      And steady through the waves.

A rising note on lighted voice:
No one to act or make the choice:
      Nobody to be saved!

DEATH BY WATER

The wave: the swelling of—and crowning crest
And crashing of—viridian upon
White bloated sails exchanging wind for wash.
Mold-eaten planks fall crumbled underneath
The moon's full night, as bones fall shattered by
The moon's full light. The flesh, as loose as sails,
Bleeds lures toward the famished fish. The tooth
Retrieves its gifts and revels down toward
Unreckoned depths. The Lady's veil accepts
And lowers all toward her lap; with grace
Of self-assurance she brings down, and hymns,
By hidden tides, the memories of one
Aboard: an echo written in her skin
Informing his upcoming life. The man

In many pieces drifts across the rocks
And crabs; the crabs from many places come
And snatch: the claw, and pinching jaw, and then
The feast of meat and cloth, until alone
The currents burnish the last fragments of
His bones: the cleanliness of womb-time found
Again by pallid stones. The Lady chants
And summons him upward, his soul, out of
The sand. She has prepared a boat for him,
A single-sail bateau that he will man
Toward the recent-drowned, and taking them
Aboard ensure their travel overseas,
Over the Undersea of her wide lap,
And waves, the swelling ones, and crashing down . . .

THE NIGHT'S FALL

A wind across the balcony: I score the city lights:
How promising when following the patterns so precisely!
How frivolous to move what moves already of its own!
Who will remember what had never been known?
Who will remember and repeat the gnashing and the singing in
    the crowded central streets,
When memory itself is overthrown?

I write these letters on the wall
And pray against another fall.
The veil is heavy that hides
The earth's recording shawl.

What prayer will wrap that shawl around our shoulders?
What tongue will utter the inscriptions?
What silence will allow each one to hear?
And where is it found? And how is it shared?

No god can break the actions of a god.
The Will is One that moves the waters,
Always free. So I have learned to watch . . .

And while diseases eat our bodies, and daggers tunnel into
    hearts,
And the fleeing are constrained by wanting bread and wanting
    water,
And by the want of play beneath the sprinklers of childhood
    memories,
And by the remembering only of one name, and the forgetting of
    histories,
A blinded man who smiles by night as brightly as by day

The Word

Goes tapping a steady rhythm along the sidewalks though
   knowing:
Many will die. Many will live as dead. No soul will there remain.

I press my eyes against the images of gardens.
Let us move our bodies in the fields
And gather up seed and stone to shield
Our green growing, and let us never harden.

Now should we take our seedlings to the streets
And learn to nurture them inside of potholes?
Or guard within our strict protection,
Later to throw their petals from the balustrade?

I do not know where the waxwings went in the winter,
Or whether they'll return to meet our shame.
I stand beside the mesh with the torn holes,
In case the flies come, welcoming,
And looking onward from the balcony,
With hazel eyes to watch the falling rain.

Act III: The Dying

Scattered riots:
The smoke above the fires
Plumes the bare trees.

The Word

In summer's garden
The choked weeds break—
Rabbit ears keep still.

Act III: The Dying

Summer's heavy stillness—
The plum leaf flutters
At the wind of my song.

A ZUCCHINI LEAF AFTER A SUMMER RAIN

Your underside glows as the burn of emerald embers:
The freshness of your infancy, exposed to us
In shaping yourself round into a water bowl.
How serenely you hold the rain that danced
Against your surface till each droplet flowed to rest!
How serenely you hold the insect resting
Within a patch of rays the sun has given you!

The insect drinks of your abundance, a little,
Among the speckles of white dust
That powder your sun-darkened skin.
Do you feel the white dust? Do you hurt?
While wavering yet doubtless in the wind?

Act III: The Dying

The midsummer sunset,
A wisp on the winds of my memory—
The playground laughter.

DEATH BY AIR

The wind, capricious breath, testing its own
Ingredients, enshrouds the climber of
The foothills of the Mount at Middleland:
A welcome waft to lighten weights upon
Long-trudging feet, and kindly lift the feet
Above the ground. The ground, receding fast,
Becomes the longing of the man, and yet
A fearful thing to meet while spinning round
And round the head, as atmosphere makes doll
Of him who cannot breathe to scream. The lungs
Deprived quickly of gaseous drink—they shrink,
And don't expand, and freeze where leaking heat
Runs scarce. The final breath blows out and joins
Itself unto the playful one. The breath

Of man at last relieved of marrow and
Of bile—he watches all drop limp and swift
Below, and hit, and splatter out, the fluids
As free as breath on wind. So man achieves
His eagle hope of Middle Mountain's high
Summit; although so cheated of the climb
And thorough suffering, he carries still
His threadbare memories, which haunt, and draw
From rest. He wrestles with the wind downward,
And desperately directs the current to
One journeying as yet, enswathing first
The shoulders then the legs and weary feet,
The breath-assembly moving now as one.
The wind, as eagle-gyre, uplifts again . . .

A WITHERED ROSE

Scarlet petals curling into purple lips,
Your satin touch reverts to that of dust.
Pale leaves enshroud your thornless stem
Reaching above the stone vase rim,
At ease amid the loud and silent rushing.
Upon your vase your hardened cousin grows
Out of a rock where the winds rise and fall
With the moon's nightly call. Each knows
Your presence but forgets; and without minds
To rearrange there are no hands to mangle.
No wind will bellow in the basement here;
The planet's pull can pull no stronger.
Firm in your austere fragility, you remind us:
How effortless is death: how deathless beauty.

The Word

Shredded family photographs—
The camp guards' rollicking obeys
The Will of the Lord.

THE BODY

Flame-bearer wrought of stone and sea!
O you who fan the kindling with the meadow-breath:
Pirouette your elements as Earth around the Fire,
Which, never born to matter, never tastes of shadow-death.

Pirouette your elements on buoyancy of mirth!
Let spill the little flame! As often in your youth,
When those who shivered fully shawled
Had thawed their eyelids at your hearth.

What devastating splendor! Fitting crown!
When they had lifted you to dawn!
Within what subtle twitch had they betrayed
Their hearts' thick envy—O how they had drawn

The ink of shame across your surfaces!
Observe the speed of nerves as honest witnesses!
And I believed the writings that you wore.
And I unlearned of you, forgetting the before.

And what stern valleys have I carved across your brow!
What passion for redemption! How many peddled crafts!
How credible the blade and draping cloth!
The shaken drink that scrapes at every draft!

What recompense were rare and anxious laughs?
Except when will fell still, and belly-honest roars
Engraved the sketches on your cheeks,
Restoring to your face a little symmetry.

Except on mountain stone and waving sea,
When you revealed the valor of your form:

The Word

To touch the pulsing roots! To drink the surging charge!
To effortlessly leap upon a cloud!

O fire-thrower: ferry forth that charge
Upon the lightness of winged feet!
O they have asked for us on silver!
O they begin with you, at first a sliver!

Run the rivers ever in their steadiness
Upon this planet of the poisoned breath!
What of a little more of poison?
You have shown worthiness of rest.

At the appointed time we will depart:
You unto the womb, and I the Unknown.
May you receive an honored sepulchre:
And revel in the glory of the worms!

DEATH BY FIRE

Flame, bursting, born in its death, as it wraps
The stake and body, gives its glow to that
Pale flesh. The flesh alighting—firms—then slacks,
Then plays the lick, wearing the lick as fine
Linen, diaphanously flowing. So
By way of heat; so, fully, by the light-
Path, and encircled by the martyrs, held
Also within the flame (however un-
Burnt); so, bleeding, and blood steaming, and blood
Becoming gas as fire, an offering
To Heaven, the enfolded one, rapt, breathes
Out—cry upon cry—cry upon the smoke
And lifting. And the one consumed becomes,
Amid the burning, him—the One, and All

In all—in rising to that frequency.
The risen ones are waiting: outstretched palms
And arms, wide, pulsing, and electric: songs
And colors emanating: hues and tones
Soon blanketing. Where fire finds its source, there,
Unknown, except by Spirit, there Soul perceives
And learns new ways; there Soul can imitate
And, practicing the song, can, at last, know
The Old Way, and remember the Old Self-
Hood. There is magic in the Self, creates
And renews. Known, knowing, exacting too,
The patterns reemerge on Earth, and spark
A last Becoming, Earth herself fulfilled.
Flame, blazing, born of new death, turns the gyre . . .

A PLUM TREE AT SUMMER'S END

A yellow leaf has fallen to the grass;
And sepia with rot along the edges,
It wavers on the still-green blades. The wind
Has freshened as the moons have come and passed,
Attended by a waltzing pair of stars.
The wind has basked the lesser underneath
Our sentry star, withdrawing early now
To take its rest. And you perceive the change
And let your leaves onto the wind; and lose
Your leaves entirely in time. You lose
Before the fruits have grown and fallen split
Upon your roots. And now the wasps are fewer,
Unable to find sugar in the rot that lines
Your stems, consuming you entirely in time.

Act III: The Dying

Harvest eve—
Candles scattered skyward
Tire, and are smothered.

The Word

A fallen flower
Consumed within the fire
Of fallen leaves.

THE RIVER GIRL

I met a girl along the river overturning wetted pebbles
And examining the crayfish shells against the shrouded sun.
I asked her if she had discovered any with the azure shells;
She reached into her satchel and she told me, "Only one."
She pulled out of her satchel a dilapidated shell,
Which, even through the haze, once hit by midday light,
Turned radiant with hues of unremembered shallow seas.
I asked her, "Had your purpose been to find the sea-toned
    shells?"
She stowed the shell inside her satchel, turned her sealike eyes to
    mine,
And, rising to my waist in height, spoke straightly unto me:

"I have come looking for my mother. Have you seen my mother?
Underneath the river's pebbles or upon the current's crests?
I have not seen her under mosses or upon the sparrows' wings.
I lost her in the bombings. Were you at the bombings?
When metal void of mysteries was thrown upon the earth
And shattered into bullets that destroyed onlooking eyes?
While horses stuck with spurs had trampled down the shouting
    crowds?
And bulls enraged with spurs had pierced the runners of the
    crowds?
And all the city fell inverted, at the shaking of the plates,
And the volcanoes threw up ashes, turning all the city gray?
Had you been present also?"

I said I had been present, though I had not seen her mother,
And that I had also lost somebody when the city turned to gray.
I had been drawn toward a light above the flying bombers,
Attention which preserved my sight; though in that time she
    disappeared,

The Word

The one I kept a watch on, and I did not see which way.
The river girl suggested that we amplify our vision
By walking with our hands conjoined throughout the ashy mist.
She crossed the rocks and took my hand
Along a fern-abounding path,
A little skip within her step, and meanwhile saying this:

"I understand your trouble, losing someone in your watch.
It is the same with me: I am my mother's keeper.
And I have come to guide her soul throughout the final fall,
As she had done for me in other earthly lives.
And yet how much the harder as we reach the final fall!
When bloodless demons prick our veins, and magnets spin our hearts,
And ancient maps cannot be read when we cannot find north.
How easily a word is thrown at overpassing planes!
And at the unbelieving playing orchestrated games.
Even the remembering get pulled into collapse.
That's when my mother went from me,
While singing in her wandering,
But I no longer heard her song amid the growing din.
And I no longer saw her once I had forgone my sight.
We keepers have to keep ourselves within a steady peace."

We came at length upon a cliff that dropped into a valley:
Across us stood a pallid horse on the opposing wall,
A hooded rider on his back:
And horse and rider both had cast their shadow on the valley.
Beneath that steely shadow, greenery turned yellow, and
The bounty of the trees all writhed against their withering—
Uncovering a golden glow emitting from the earth below.
The river girl then said to me, "Remember this new Eden,
When you have found again the soul within your watch.
And move to here with haste: there may be time for running.
And do receive the blessings of the valley's knowing guard.
This Eden will serve host unto our cycle's last Becoming."

Act IV:

The Becoming

MARCHING

Ablaze had burst the Spirit on the water,
Fully wasting yesterworld through the smoke,
The flames exploding out of fountains.
Aright had set the Motions the dry land
In symmetry of ridges and of delves
Against the fruiting of the sea.

We walk those paths that we had walked with angels,
Before the breaking of the land and crooked angles,
And wonder at the last if we must walk alone.
The moon has not abandoned us; that orb is only resting.
The stars have not abandoned us; they still shine forth their
    blessings.
Though we are slow of reading what we once had known.

Our bodies, wheeling, move their course regardless,
For who among us can deny his body's movements?
And who among us claims to be so real as to act?
And so our stepping, written for us long before our age,
Runs steadily throughout the mire of our adopted fears.

We pass again across this world, a poised and smoking stage.
The only place that we can meet is our appointed home.

The Word

Wire-guarded pond—
A bud-studded branch rests
On spring ice.

ACT IV: THE BECOMING

Wind-worn nest,
The trilling of the fledgling—
A gust plucks a feather.

The Word

Beach-breaking forest:
The water bend disappears—
Gaps in leaves sparkle.

THE ARGUMENT

*On the march to Eden, two men grown tired with evening engage
in argument, and are answered by a third.*

"The fruit had peeled our lids and honed our eyes!
We saw—the first to see!—the tree-cast shades
That crept with winds over our naked flesh.
We witnessed first the cover-piercing rays
That warmed our blood to striving! Now, though, fruitless,
And withered, we return at will to ignorance?"

"The fruit had blinded us with ignorance.
The snake had called it wisdom. Focused eyes
Will strain at stones and call a garden fruitless.
Do you perceive the value of the shades?
Do you believe you could withstand the rays
In full, although they be contained within our flesh?"

"We have been granted weakness of the flesh
And would be weakest in our ignorance
Among our fellow beasts. Respect the rays
Of human intellect; or close your eyes,
Yet still you will catch cold beneath the shades.
A sickly body you will have, one small and fruitless."

"Our bodies we have long since rendered fruitless,
When we believed we could improve on flesh
And sought for answers in the murmuring shades.
Willingly we have welcomed ignorance
And held too proudly to our earthly eyes.
We once had wisdom, when we watched the dawning rays."

"Do you deny the brightening of the rays?

The Word

Will you deny a bounty? Turn it fruitless?
I will not join you. I have trained my eyes
And by collective wit enhanced my flesh.
I've fought against the sways of ignorance.
I do not willingly abide among the shades!"

"The light you praise is tinted by the shades.
You have forgotten the original rays.
Your knowledge only shows your ignorance,
And so your exaltations follow fruitless.
I do deny the failings of the flesh—
For light; since I have seen with eyes beyond my eyes!"

—"All eyes perceiving only ignorance,
In shades or light, by bounty or the fruitless,
We walk as one: the flesh itself as heaven's rays."

Act IV: The Becoming

Desiccated leech—
The shroud of mist evaporates
At dawn.

The Word

Blushing blossoms burst
Between the rotted tumors
On the wide, still lake.

Act IV: The Becoming

Fallen branch—
Even the sun-touched sword
Passes through.

TO THE VILLAINS AT FULFILLMENT

Villains! Oathbreakers!
Thrashers of flesh and of laws!
Crashers of cities with bombs!
Idle-promisers of fortunes!
Thieves of mighty fortunes!
Binders of mothers to warriors!
Cleavers of thinkers from fathers!
Breeders of guilt in the worthy!
Feeders of shame to the stout!
Forgers of histories!
Seamsters of loathing and doubt!
Drinkers of pus of the youth!
Diners on corpses of youth!
Spreaders of glitches through minds!
Maestros of glitching new minds!
Hard-hearted and iron-helmed!
Silken-tied and whitened-smiling!
Mesmerizers!
And mesmerized—

May you receive the mercy of the embers
Which you have stoked from nails in long Novembers.
May ashes light with favor on your brows
And singe the final flaking of your shrouds.
May the White Light, director of the scenes,
Animator of public and unseen
Performances by you and by us all—
May that our Guide, amid this closing fall
And novel rising, bring you from your tombs
Into this atmosphere, and through these fumes,
To meet us your kin. For you have breathed together;
Let us all now breathe together. There's a feather

Act IV: The Becoming

Upon the wind that follows as we walk.
Follow the feather to us; let us not talk
Much longer. Come! Come with us to Becoming!
Those with the feather have no need of running.
Come now! So at arrival you may bow
Before forgiving clapping of the crowd,
For having played your roles so expertly.
Come! Come and witness what is next to be
Upon this plane! Come see the Appointer's face
And live! Engulfed in gratitude and grace.

TO THE YOUTHFUL AT FULFILLMENT

Newly souled and lava-shod!
Call-receivers shawled in your first sea-foam mist!
Heavy is the fall! How do you miss before-time's lightness?
Lightness you have brought us in your blossoming through
    wreckage!
Joyous shone your smiling through the clasp of cloying shades!
Hopeful have you clambered up toward your golden summits,
    shouting new veracities upon the gelded glades!
Observe how true words plummet!

What snares, however, caught you while ascending foothill paths?
What cunning keeps you so enthralled within your own
    intentions?
At last! As quick the climbing up the mount, so quick the coming
    down!
And now the gold has cooled from its liquid into iron.
And now deceits are laid across the meadows for our witness.
The challenge of the Witness! Learning heavy as the fall . . .

Young-flaming, take no jading from the elders bending backs
    beneath their burdens: take neither opinion from the elders lost
    of wisdom!
For many lives were needed; many lives you may need also, as
    you build upon the burdens gathered, loaded, on your backs—
The burdens which you may abandon ever at your will!
But if you must hold on, then hold on lightly.
And watch your own perfection, errors folding into purpose.
Fulfillment is achieved: may you return or cycle on, with blessings
    on your head, protected always by your sheath!

TO THE ANCIENTS AT FULFILLMENT

Ancients of ages among us: you first builders
Who shuffle through your ruins, downward looking:
Do you remember sunlight's dawning, casting
All shadows from the earth by way of flooding?
So much has been forgotten through the cycling.
Do you remember forest's giving, fruiting
Of exaltation? Birds had sung as sweetly
Before the learning of long lamentation.
What cause had shaken the breathing's melodies?
Before land-rending wars, engulfing seas,
What heart-held whispers marred the noon of peace?
So much has been forgotten through the falling.

For long you have been grasping at the fading
Of reminiscences, retrieving threading
To serve as teachings: meanwhile ever delving,
And vaster, through material affairs—
Until the losing of the tapestry,
Evaporating as a morning dream.
And minds began the seeking, hands achieving,
Sweetness less sweet, and joy less joyous: making
Of imitations and degenerating,
Working eventually brutality
Itself into the stone for emulating.
So much has been forgotten through the clambering—

Until your souls, alight with the alarming,
Within this age of self-deception, spurring
Your bodies through their motions—souls remember
Within the flaming depths within their centers
That there can be no loss where there's no gain:
That even iron glistens golden sheen.

The Word

Ancients! Release what you could never hold!
For we are not the doers: we are Witness.
And all has been devised for your fulfillment,
As you have always known from the beginning.
Now at the glowing end may you refold
In golden shining, biding always still
Inside the axis, or, at your decision,
Descend again to dawn a golden scene!

TO THE PROPHETS AT FULFILLMENT

For Marc Di Saverio

Prophets! At last! Lay down your prophecies!
See how they now take form among the stars!
Bow silent hearts before theophanies!

Your words had struck out all apostasies
And cleaved with verve the darkening that mars
Prophets. At last! Lay down your prophecies

As you had laid away your oddities
And lightless ways that held you as formless bars!
Bow silent hearts before theophanies!

What urge is there to speak when honesties
Walk with us in the masks of your memoirs?
Prophets, at last! Lay down your prophecies!

As you had given your tongues to God who sees
Your striving, give the spirit that still spars!
Bow silent hearts before theophanies!

And cast your shells to the forgotten seas:
Allow the final healing of your scars!
Prophets! At last! Lay down your prophecies!
Bow silent hearts before theophanies!

THE BECOMING

Our footing failing by the garden where the leaves, half-chewed,
    have yellowed,
And bumblebee, a static shell, sleeps pollenless on wilted petals,
And twine has caught the bowing stem to capture dimming
    dignity,
We gather at our meeting place at ending of our history.

The glistening within each eye reflects the glare beneath all mist,
And guides our last desires toward fulfilling the eternal wish.
Do you perceive within your mind the stirs of ancient memories?
Affix your gaze to glistening when bearing pain of memory!

Release the ashes and the relics of your children gone to storms!
Abandon coats and photographs! You have no further need for
    warmth.
Observe the speeding of the wind: disturbing trees of stately rest.
Observe the speeding of the patterns beating louder in your
    chest!

Within the glade, atop this rock, at center of this dusking vale,
The spirit shades begin to talk in form of mothers' cutting wails:

Our selves, our own! Our love's creation!
Abandoned wholly to destruction—
Bastards, all, who have split our throats
And bled us over dear cremations!
How can we draw the breath that reeks of offered babes?
How can we drink the stream that runs with ruby stains?
How can we bite the bread imbued with ashen flakes?
How can we flee or linger, weltering, within this waste?

Act IV: The Becoming

"Hear!" shout the speakers from across the stricken crowd,
And posturing upon the scatterings of rock,
With fist upheld to chest, or book upon the wrists,
They swell their lungs and fall to moss in silence,
As the wind throws their answers back into their mouths.
This is no hour for reciting.

The forest borders start their waking,
As shades detach from trunks of trees
And move with stillness at their knees.
The debt collectors have arrived
In raven cloaks that graze the earth,
Beyond earth's measuring of worth,
Enlarging their apparent size.
This is the hour of their taking.

Black hounds in growing growling chorus
Appear from underneath the cloaks,
And herd us gathered tighter, circling,
Their tracks a wheel, their stares the spokes;
With the moon in their eyes they force us
Beneath the center of the whirling
Within the sky, the dusty stars
Close, twirling, in a threatening splendor—

The hounds release from tracking, leaping, howling, for the masses,
And fang a maiden's necklace, bite the pendant into shards,
And claw and crash the frames and glass of an old merchant's glasses,
And slip a wedding band and hold it nimbly in the jaw.
And who would not give up the ring would lose the finger also.
And who had grasped the glasses, after then no longer saw.
And who withheld the necklace felt the pierce where chests are tender.

The Word

And with the rounding up of all the lush and dainty falsehoods,
Retrieved into the cloaks that wait along the shadowed rim,
The hounds return to take from us the things the less material:
The tongue that flicks out curses, or the lips that hum a hymn,
Are torn away from faces, leaving gaping purple holes;
And thoughts of fleeing prick the hounds perceiving the ethereal,
Who lunge and rend that portion from the overactive skulls.
And hatred harbored in the hearts is taken with the hearts.

And some the hounds take whole by dragging ankles through the dirt.
And how the dragged ones scream! How desperate their searching eyes
For help among the sufferers: how useless outstretched hands!
No one can take the hold against the wrath of forest hounds.
The trying fall, the weakened crawl, the decimated lie.
And those untouched are those who give up their possessions freely,
Who sit in silence, closing eyes, beneath the stars still wheeling.

And when the silent have achieved their state of perfect silence,
A light within their easy hearts emits through see-through flesh
And spreads toward the gentle mourners and toward the scathing,
Igniting flames to soften hearts and turn the scales to mesh.
And some release their mourning and allow the lighting through;
And others fight the impulse spilling clear where hounds had chewed,
And then collapse to earth beneath the weight of silence bathing,
And cease their breathing with the ceasing of the garden violence.

The hounds retreat to cloaks and merge with shadows.
The debt collectors wrap their swollen cloaks
In many layers, turning then to fade
To forest blackness. Wide-leaf canopies—
The forest being nourished by the payments—

Act IV: The Becoming

Extend their heights to heaven's blanketing,
Appearing so to touch the sparkling gyre.
The moon in fullness hangs within the center.
Within the core of every silent one,
The lighting grows in radiance and casts
Their open veins against the towering leaves,
As though a film projected on a screen.
And in a moment of eternity,
The drama of our history plays out,
Recounting all in rich detail and truth:

The golden morning and initial glory
Of mankind's entry on this planet's stage;
The revels in the garden—earthly angels—
Before the need for keeping memories:

The fissure from the Source, and the creation
Of the Other, when though split we still perceived
The many flowerings of our Source-sparked souls
And built tremendously by silver light:

The further falling into flowerings;
Identities with beauteous petals—O!
How wonderful these gifts that we protected,
Stirring in copper pots, and how unstable:

The severing, as delicate petals blown
By hurried winds; the landing in the mud,
And working then of iron for our climbing;
The loneliness within the lonely sty:

The seasons of the ages so performed
Until the very moment of our watching,
This very moment of the cycle's ending,
The gyre above begins the showering
Of ivory-petaled lilies on the heads

The Word

Of all those present: petals which repair
The hound-inflicted wounds and stanch the bleeding:
Petals erasing traumas, reinforcing
Seams between brothers who had long averted
Their eyes, and meet their eyes again, embracing:
Petals uniting families split by pain,
Who hear each other's hearts again, embracing:
Until all stand enshrouded in the shining
Of starlit lilies, hands supporting hands,
And starlit eyes streaming and skyward aiming.

The pebbles at our feet awake to trembling, lifting lightly from the earth to hang about us in the air.
And blood inside our veins awakes to surging, swelling the pulsing inside our brains, our thoughts cycloning.
And birds reverse directions in the skies.
Our glade awakes to growing to a mountain, making valleys of the mountains that surrounded us.
And lily light beams as a beacon overland and calls all corpses from their ashes and all dancers from their dances.
And light undoes the gripping—glasses shatter on the earth, and palms arise to shield the eyes, and bodies clamber under stones.
The light consumes the all as famished flames that sweep the forest.
And light uplifts the all as smoke that floats upon the fires,
Until the light alone is seen across inverted land,
Until the truth of light is all remaining to be known.
And we look back on history as long and weary journeys cherished and forgiven at the welcome of our home:
Millennia of dust that bring the second hand to rust:
This moment that is still and without ticking.
All the lives lived do not compare;
The many miles crossed are not the width of a hair.

O Veil who sow all covers' questioning,
You woven with earthly threads and heavenly,

Act IV: The Becoming

Who lead the kindled by your ley lines: you
Always in pattern with remembering
Who close the light inside of human hearts
To pressurize and burst through angel voices—

O Speaker of these words on lighted voices
And Animator of all questioning,
Who fan the longing in the kindled hearts
And move these hands to build the heavenly:
You Keeper of the vast remembering:
Ten thousand forms, expressions only of you—

O Light of Silence! Light of Stillness: you
Upholding every form yet void of voices,
Empty of dust and of remembering,
Needless of answers to the questioning:
You beyond even what is heavenly,
Residing always in the bodiless Heart—

O you who hear this prayer within the Heart—
O you who meet your endings at the start—
O you released from markings in the sand—
At last I know just who and what: I am

www.ingramcontent.com/pod-product-compliance
Lightning Source LLC
Chambersburg PA
CBHW071717040426
42446CB00011B/2100

9798385207428